To Virginia

SEEKING JESUS

A Meditation for ever … n
prayer, poetry, prose, and …

COLIN FERGUSON

ISBN 978-0-9566519-0-7

Printed and bound in Great Britain by
www.direct-pod.com

…………………………………………………………………………

Thanks be to God who constantly makes us think about what we are doing. Help us we pray, to always seek how we can become the people that God would like us to be.

SEEKING JESUS

A collection of prayers, poems, reflection and meditation, across the year that seeks the presence of Christ in every day, every one and every where. Praise God for his gifts and for the words with which he has blessed me. Colin

The collection is based on the revised Common Lectionary and is suitable either for personal prayer and meditation or for use in Worship.
Starting in Advent, there is an entry for each potential week. As the lectionary covers a three year cycle, the various lengths of Lent and Pentecost are covered. Some entries will relate to a theme such as One World Week, others to a lectionary passage relating to the week

Cover picture – Morning shower (by Colin Ferguson)

Enquiries to **Colin Ferguson, 20 Matlock Road, Caversham, Reading, RG4 7BS**
Telephone 0118 9482557
email colindf@btinternet.com

Contents

Epiphany 7 Where it hurts

Transfiguration Surprising God

Epiphany 8 God Slob
(Published in the United Reformed Church Prayer Handbook 1998 – Active Power)

Lent 1 Commandment

Lent 2 Tempted / On giving things up

Lent 3 Debt – Broken Jaw

Lent 4 Mother God

Passion Communion
(Published in 'Let Justice Roll Down – Canterbury Press 2003 and Sounds of Fury – United Reformed Church 1994)

Palm Sunday Why me?
(Published in the United Reformed Prayer Handbook 2000 – Justice, Joy and Jubilee)

Good Friday Simon of Cyrene
(Published in 'Let Justice Roll Down'-Canterbury Press 2003)

Easter Saturday Nightmare
(Published in the United Reformed Church Prayer Handbook 1998 – Active Power)

Easter Sunday Four step
(Published in Let Justice Roll Down – Canterbury Press 2003)

Easter Monday Be not afraid

Easter 2 Thomas

Easter 3 Fishermen

Easter 4 With sadness

Easter 5 (Christian Aid Week) Hungry Child / Bus stop

Easter 6 Friends

Easter 7 When God says No

Ascension day Coming down the mountain
(Published in the United Reformed Church Prayer Handbook 2000 Justice, Joy and Jubilee)

Pentecost Wake up Christian
(Published in Worship Live - Issue 16 – 2000)

Trinity Travellers

Pentecost 2 Preacher's prayer

Pentecost 3 That's not me!

Pentecost 4 Refugee
(Published in 'Let Justice Roll Down'- Canterbury Press 2003)

Pentecost 5 Giants
(Published in the United Reformed Church Prayer Handbook 1998 – Active Power.)

Pentecost 6 Comfort zone

Pentecost 7 Who is my neighbour?

Pentecost 22 All Saints
Bella
(Published in Entertaining Angels – Canterbury Press 2005)

Pentecost 23 Christian Foolishness

Pentecost 24 Cenotaph

Pentecost 25 Caged Earth
(Published in Worship the King- Marshall Pickering 1992)

Pentecost 26 Doing my best

Pentecost 27 Patience

Pentecost 28 Rainbow and the Berlin wall

Healing service Stand up

Prayer for the year Every

Advent 1 Ding Dong

It's Christmas time again and the streets are full of people.
There are glittering decorations overhead;
music is playing goodwill to all
and bells are ringing from the steeple,
but the crowds rush by, their prayers unsaid.

It's Christmas time again and the shops are selling madly,
while carols played by the Round Table
in the High Street call for peace to all.
The child on the poster looks on sadly
as they rattle their collection tins around a plastic stable.

It's Christmas time again and the cash is flowing freely;
the celebrations carry on heedless
and the loudspeaker blares out love to all..
The child has eyes that can only see
a pain and a hunger that were needless.

It's Christmas time again and in the midst of plenty
the bells are jingling on the shops cash till
and herald angels sing of mercy to all.
Her heart and stomach remain empty
of peace, mercy, love or goodwill

It's Christmas time again and they do not see her.
How do we teach those who have passed her by
that the child is no longer a stranger,
for when we sing justice for all,
or goodwill and peace, or mercy and love, we cry
glory for this child as well as the child in the manger.

Advent 2 Christmas Letter (Philipp. 1)

We have just written our Christmas letter Lord,
the one we send to distant friends and relations each year
to let them know what has been happening .
Then we wondered what letter our church might write!
Or worse still what you might write to us!!
What would you say?

Dear Christians, or My Dear Friends,
Perhaps, My Dearly Beloved Friends,
or more likely you would just say Oh Dear!
Would your heart be full of joy at what we have done?
    How we have helped to spread your good news?
    How we have grown in grace?
Would you have a special place in your heart
because of the way that we have shared in your pain
as well as your good times?
In your Good Friday as well as your Christmas?

Dear Lord, help us in all we do
to celebrate your coming into the world by showing
your loving kindness and compassion to each other,
by speaking freely about your great love for us
and by living in a way that shows we mean what we say.
    Teach us how to grow in your Spirit
    so that our lives may overflow with your love
    and be an example of what is right and good.
Show through the middle of the hubbub
that is called Christmas today,
our witness to your presence at the very heart of life ,
so that, when people see what we do, they praise your name
Then Lord we might joyfully write to you and sign ourselves
Yours Faithfully

Advent 3 **Coming soon**

Wonderful God, we give you thanks for the promise of Jesus
and we praise you because joy fills our lives
and tumbles into the world
as people hear the Christmas story.
We give you thanks for those who tell the good news
and share your love with those they meet.
Thanks for those who teach us and prepare us for our life pilgrimage;
for those whose joy is never squashed
by the misfortunes of life;
for those who have cherished us in our past
and led us to know you as God.
For those whose guidance and faith
has inspired and guided us
and prepared our way for us.
Glory be to God.

Yet with all our praise and thankfulness Lord
we still get things wrong
and do what you would not want us to do,
and we fail to do the work that you would like us to do.

Forgive us we pray when our faith wobbles
and our hope is short sighted.
Forgive us when we limit our love and withhold our joy.
Forgive us when we are not at peace with one another,
when we have no patience with those
who look at life differently.
Forgive us when we do not forgive.
Love us when we do not love as you would like us to.
Forgive us we pray
and prepare us to be the people you would like us to be

Advent 4 Empowering Mary

I am not often surprised by what happens but when a woman on the other end of an aisle in Waitrose suddenly squealed my name and rushed up to me and grabbed me in an affectionate hug and kissed me, I was a bit nonplussed and the staff seemed quite amused. Fortunately I did recognise her.

Mary didn't stay long but said that I had saved her life some fifteen years ago by giving her such wonderful support and encouragement when she had been at the point of killing herself because life had become so awful. Now she was free from her brutal husband, her children were grown up and she was running a shelter for women who had suffered as she had done. Then she was gone, thanking me as she went and blowing a final kiss down the aisle.

I did remember her and she was indeed a changed person. When I had known her she was pregnant and on her own with two young children in very sub standard accommodation. Her husband had recently gone to prison leaving her with massive debts. His treatment of her had resulted in the loss of any friends and most of her family. She had been truly alone and in desperate circumstances.

Although I helped by getting some early financial support and some new furniture to replace the goods taken by the bailiffs, most of what I did was to support her in going to the right places to sort out for herself what needed to be done to help her have control over her own life. It was a long and slow process, not helped when she lost her baby.

She was only on probation for a year but I continued to see her for about six months beyond that just to make sure she was able to cope. When she was moved to decent accommodation I lost contact, until that kiss!

Christmas **The Carpenter**

I wonder what he thought, the carpenter,
who took his Mary for a bride
in spite of her unlikely tale,
who took as son the unknown child
along the dangerous Bethlehem trail and loved him as his own.

I wonder how he felt, the carpenter,
as she lay in the stable
calling to God in her birth pain;
was he delivering the baby,
wrapping him up and laying him on the grain, nursing them as his own.

I wonder what he thought, the carpenter,
when shepherds and then wise men came
telling him their amazing tales,
bringing gifts and praising the baby's name,
warning them to leave that day for Egypt, on their own.

I wonder what he felt, the carpenter,
as Jesus grew and learned the tales
that Mary told him day by day,
while Joseph worked to keep them safe
and raised the child to honour God and pray, loving him as his own.

I wonder what he thought, the carpenter,
with this strange child within his home,
as through the years he carved and hewed
and taught him all that he had known,
raising him to the shapes of wood as if they were his own.

Sunday after Christmas **God M.B.E**

I find that as I get older the honours list seems to have little importance. I don't even know what I would do if I was offered one, though I know what my wife would tell me to do with it. It is however highly unlikely. Anyway, what would I do with it? Stick it in a cupboard or flaunt it. I already have some letters that I can put after my name which I rarely use except in weak moments of bravado. I find that a degree in Criminal Justice is a great put off at parties.

Honour does not seem to be a word used any more but it is still there. It is sad though that dishonour sells more newspapers and goodness doesn't. In my youth I worked in the Bank of England and there was a strong code of honourable behaviour. The stock exchange motto was '*My word is my bond*' and I have tried to live up to that ever since though the city does not seem to take it seriously any more.

Maybe my early reading influenced me. Even the comics I read (and you could read them in those days) were of honourable characters. Not surprisingly I loved the Arthurian legends. Going to church made sense to me because this was the place for honourable people and Christ was the ultimate sacrificial hero.

Jesus made sense to me. He gave honour to everyone he met whether they deserved it or not. He gave people a sense of personal value which the world denied them. His greatest act of honour was to give his life because of the great love that God has for us. God gives us honour, and it is God that we honour by what we do, especially as we too give honour to those around us and give their lives the true value that has been freely given to us.

January 1st **New year revolutions**

It often takes a child to challenge one's perception and when my youngest son told me he had made a New Year revolution he unintentionally gave it a much more challenging concept. After all what are resolutions which don't have any real resolve to them.

Often it is simple common sense. I do not need to be a prophet to know that the behaviour patterns of many young people will have terrible consequences for them in the future, far worse than just a hangover in the morning.

Already the number of teenagers being treated for alcoholism and drug addiction is at record levels, especially among young women and the number of sexually transmitted diseases is worse than it has ever been including AIDS. For a moment's 'fun' lives can be marred for ever.

Perhaps now is the time to recall the words of Deuteronomy:-
I am now giving you the choice between life and death, between God's blessing and God's curse, and I call heaven and earth to witness the choice you make. Choose life. (Deuteronomy 30 vs. 19)

This is what God wants us to do, to choose life, choose the things that will make life better for ourselves and for others and for the whole of creation. Most importantly we can show young people that there is a value to life.

For ourselves we only need to think of what we want to be doing this time next year to appreciate the changes we need to make. It is life that is God's most precious gift to us and it is up to each of us how we make the best of it. We don't need half hearted resolutions, but we might need a revolution. May God bless this coming year and help us to choose the life he would like us to have.

Christmas 2 **Forgive us for Christmas**

Lord God!
In all the pleasure this Christmas has given us
we ask for your forgiveness
for we have been so carried away by the festivity
that we forgot it was your birthday
and in our generosity to our friends and families
we made it difficult for you to be heard.

Now in the rush to buy things in the sales,
as families return to their own homes,
as we make resolutions that will not last,
as we regret the extra drink and the last mince pie,
we pray for you
to cut through all the trappings and remind us of your real message.
A child was born into a sinful and poverty stricken world
to make God known to his people,
and to love us so much
that the child whose name we praise
died for us so that we might be put right with God.

On his promise of forgiveness we depend,
On his message of salvation we rely,

Help us Lord to be your Christmas people.

Epiphany **Epiphany Prayer**

Glory be to God who has come to us.

While we have rejoiced in the stories of Christmas,
Epiphany has called us back to our daily life
and the darkness of January days
and the colds and aches of winter,
make us all too aware of our own frailty
and inclination to hide away.

But your word reminds us that we do have gifts to bring,
journeys to travel, decisions to make,
and a message of joy and newness
that cuts through the bitter winds,
that sings in the rain and snow,
that melts the ice of those who live in winter.

Lord! Help us to be alive to the warmth of your love;
to the hope of new days;
to the love of all life.

Forgive us we pray when we allow ourselves to be overcome by the world's discomfort,
when we think we have little to offer,
when we stay put and are afraid of new challenges, new ideas.
When we say that the world's need,
the call of Jesus, the love of God is nothing to do with us.

Lord! Help us to be alive to the warmth of your love;
to the hope of new days;
to the love of all life..

Epiphany 1 Yes

Praise God our Father in heaven.
Praise God revealed to us in Jesus Christ the Son.
Praise God with us today in the Holy Spirit.
Here with us as we worship, inviting us to respond,
waiting for us to open our hearts to his transforming grace.

God is waiting for us to say **yes!**

O Lord forgive us when we find it too hard
to do what you want us to do,
too difficult to understand or to accept your word, or your love.
Forgive us when we want things to be easy for us,
when we only expect good things to happen to us
and blame you when it doesn't work out that way.
Forgive us when we walk on the other side of the road from the need
of this world, afraid to get involved.
Forgive us when we only want our friends to be like us,
look like us, sound like us, think like us.
Forgive us the narrow minds that we have grown up with
and are afraid to change.

Lord grant us the courage to believe when we cannot understand,
to accept the changes you make to our lives,
to open our arms to those who seem different

As you have loved us, as you have accepted us,
as you have forgiven us and suffered what we should have suffered
so that we too may affirm our desire
to be your people.

Yes Lord! Amen

Epiphany 2 Lord's Prayer

Our Father, let your name be known and loved

Where does your time go? Your world is not static. It is always changing, moving, creating and recreating and it is good that it does so. But how in this modern day are we to make your name known and loved?

Your kingdom come, your will be done

Sadly change can also be for the worse. People become so wrapped up in themselves that they don't stop long enough to realise that you are still here and that your gifts of love, hope, peace, joy and justice are life's foundation for all time.

Yours is the kingdom the power and the glory

As we learn more of your wonders, we are tempted to talk about our power, our knowledge, our cleverness, our wealth and we hide from your real world behind Ipods and mobile 'phones, filling our minds with chatter and loud music.

Give what we need today and treat us as well as we have treated others.

The world looks for easy power, cheap thrills and miracles but it still needs to be fed and it will always need to know the love of God and we will always need forgiveness while we blame each other for what goes wrong.

Let your kingdom be known and your will be done here and now

The truth is that we are the body of Christ, and it is we who must serve his kingdom, we who are both tempter and tempted who speak of Christ today in his world of change and challenge. It is through us that his kingdom will come.

Lead us not into temptation and deliver us from evil.

Help us to walk in the power of your kingdom and to always keep the glory of your love before us forever.

Epiphany 3 Unrecognised

The Spirit of the Lord is upon me –

It's nice to see a local lad doing well but he was always a clever one, always asking awkward questions. You wouldn't think that of a carpenter's lad, would you?

Because he has chosen me –

I blame his mother. She was always putting fancy ideas into his head. Still he has done well. Everyone is impressed with the way he teaches. It has a real sense of authority about it.

To bring good news to the poor –

That'll be the day. Perhaps he can turn these stones into bread and feed us or can he tell me how to win the lottery.

To proclaim liberty to the captives –

O yes! I can just see him trying to persuade the Romans to let their prisoners go. What sort of power does he think he has? Fine words can't unlock a cell.

To give recovery of sight to the blind –

Does he think he can undo what God has done? That he can forgive people their sins? This is Joseph and Mary's son.

To set free the oppressed –

Can you see the people rising to follow a carpenter's son? How could he drive the Romans out? He would be dead in a day and forgotten in a week.

To announce that the time has come
when God will save his people -

That won't happen in my lifetime. Jesus can't change that even with all his fine words he is still just one of us.

This has come true today as you have heard it being read

Who do you think you are Jesus? You are only a carpenter's son! Are you mad! If you speak like this we will all be killed. Go away, go away, we don't want you here. You are nothing but trouble. Go away, go away.

Epiphany 4 N.F.A.

Here John Smith lies,
laid out in style.
He was a lonely man.
No one is left to cry.
John Smith is dead,
found in a railway carriage, no fixed abode.

Euston Station, platform nine
is no place to die.
He made the trains run late
but nobody knew why.
John Smith is dead
in a London terminus, no fixed abode.

Brush his hair, comb his beard,
give him a little care.
Ten pence was in his pocket,
not enough to pay his fare.
John Smith is dead,
near the left luggage, no fixed abode

Card in a welfare cabinet,
now we can all forget
after a final priestly prayer
speeds him off with no regrets.
John Smith is dead;
blown where the wind may wish, no fixed abode.

(The 4th Sunday in Epiphany is often used for prayer for the homeless and for poverty)

Epiphany 5 **Candlemas**

l
lll
llll
lllll
llll
lll
ll
xxxxxxxxx
Candles
on a living stone,
light to shine me
home, light to show
me where to go; holy
light to help me know
what is right and what
is wrong and that people
all belong one to each other,
sisters, brothers, sons and
daughters on the move,
carrying their tents of
love, through the
darkness, desert
starkness, to the
shining of a light
in the deepest of the
night. Light within
God's living stone.
Candle
set to light me home.

Epiphany 6 When love is not enough

Len and Ellen had been married fifteen years and their three children were 11, 12 and 14 when it happened. Ellen had always been a lively woman while Len was a serious hard working man with a strong faith. Their first years of marriage had been fine because of the children but then Ellen became more and more unsettled and unfaithful.

She kept leaving and then returning briefly making no secret of the fact that she had gone with other men. Each time Len took her back.. It seemed that she had lost any care or love for her family.

She had been gone for over three months this time and the family were just beginning to settle down to a steady routine. It was 12 year old Stella's birthday and all her friends had come round for a party.

Fortunately it was nearly over when Ellen marched in through the front door turning as she did so to blow a kiss to someone outside. She was unsteady on her feet and soon made everyone in the room feel uncomfortable, so much so that Stella herself asked her friends to leave.

Len was furious, which for a normally very placid man was unusual. They were in the kitchen shouting at each other. The children heard their father shout "If you don't care about me you should at least think about our children".

His last memory of what happened was her saying back to him, "What makes you think they are your children anyway!"

He had been carving ham earlier, for the party, and the knife was next to his hand. He insisted on pleading guilty though even in his dreams he can't quite remember what he did.

Len had many friends waiting for him when he came out of prison including his now grown up children. Over seven long years had been spent in the prayers of the church to which he had always taken the family. It was still the minimum he could have done for murder and he would be on license for the rest of his life.

Though they opened their arms to welcome him home he was a man with a bad dream and a sense of guilt that never let him rest.

So often we shrink from violence failing to see it as anything to do with us. But we are all human, we do have a breaking point. It is not excusable but it is understandable. Len knew that God understood and still loved him but it would take a long time before Len would forgive himself.

Pray for the places where love has broken down.
Pray for those who must live with guilt,
and for the victims of violence especially in the home.
Pray for the children who are lost when love breaks down.

Epiphany 7 Where it hurts

How good it is to be here Lord,
here in our familiar place,
here with people we know and trust,
here where we can be apart from your world for a while,
where we can sing your praise and pray our prayers,
hear the word, and not be surprised too much.

But we know in our hearts Lord that this is an oasis
of peace and calm,
this is not your whole world ,
for you are working where it hurts,
speaking where you will be laughed at,
helping where there is little if any thanks.

And so we pray
for all whose lives are blighted;
people sick in body mind and spirit,
souls grieving in their sadness and loss,
hearts broken by deception and betrayal of love,
bodies racked by pain and disease,
spirits fettered by doubt and fear,
minds clouded by stress and disorder.

We pray for families who can no longer live together,
where love has gone and only distress and anger remain.
We pray for those who have no place to stay,
those trapped by addiction and powerlessness,
those who are lonely, feeling unloved and abandoned,
who see no future, and have no esteem for themselves.

We know Lord that you can make a difference to their lives
so help us to be your hope to the lost,
your love to the unlovable,
your light in the dark and desperate places,
your faith for those who have no future,
your joy for those who have forgotten how to smile.

Help us to be the place where you can be found,
to build a church overflowing with welcome and grace,
and help us to be the people you would like us to be,
in the name of Jesus Christ.

Transfiguration **Surprising God**

Christ of the mountain, shining in the pure light,
blessed by the presence of prophecy and law.
Suddenly your friends see you for what you are
but cannot really ever say exactly what they saw.

Christ of the high places, shining in perfection,
dazzling with majesty the minds of your close friends.
Moses and Elijah seen as your companions,
witness to the wisdom and the love that never ends.

Christ of the low places, sharing grace and glory,
touching the needy, healing the forsaken,
driving out the evil, confounding all his critics.
How in all your power could you let yourself be taken?

Christ of our history, Christ of the empty tomb,
always surprising those who follow you.
Moments of your shining light our lives for ever,
God alive within us makes our living true.

Christ of the heavens, promise of the future,
speaking to the suffering of the world today.
We are Christ in action, we today are shining,
walking in our Saviour's most surprising way.

Epiphany 8 God Slob

Oh Lord! Did you see me nodding?
I really was trying to concentrate,
especially as the preacher was talking about being prepared for the coming of Jesus.
But my mind was full of my own thoughts, my own work.
I don't plan to come to church for a rest – or do I?
Life just seems to get busier and busier
and Sunday is not different any more.
We make so little time to read the Bible,
to pray or sing,
No time except your time.
In all the time you have given us Lord,
can we not pray with you for even one hour?

Lord! Make our Sunday worship a time of vitality.
A time when we can bring together
the lives we have lived all week in your presence;
our joy at the opportunity to sing your praise;
hearts open to your word;
prayers full of belief in the power of that prayer.

Help us to give and to receive,
so that in your grace and glory
we may go out again to be your worship in the world,
to be your good news of love and peace,
hope and justice, faith and new life.
Help us to bring lives that are a worthy offering,
fit for your table.
When we are thinking of ourselves and not you Lord,
wake us up before it is too late.

Lent 1 Commandment

Lord it would be easier if you told me not to do things
as you did in the Ten Commandments,
but you have told me to love
and that is not always easy to do.

Help me to distinguish between the human soul that is in all of us
and the human behaviour which leads us to do things that are wrong,
dangerous and sometimes evil.

If only I could solve the problems of the world,
feed the hungry, clothe the naked.
If only I could do something truly amazing
that would make people listen.
But even if I ruled the world it is still just me
and the problems would return.
I would soon be forgotten,
someone else would control what happens.

It's only me Lord, trying to work out how to obey you,
how to love you with all my heart, and strength and soul;
how to love the people that you want me to love.

Help me to be your servant,
to be aware,
to be prepared,
to be willing,
to be whatever you call me to be.

With you Lord God, even I may be a sign of your salvation.

Lent 2 Tempted

Lord you know what it is like to be tempted,
especially as you had the power to change what was happening.

When we are tempted to try and solve our problems
by short term satisfaction
remind us that we do not live by bread alone.

When we are tempted to put all our problems on your shoulder
and then to blame you when they still go wrong,
remind us that we must not try to test your love.

When we are tempted to follow the crowd
and to give in to our greed and selfish nature,
remind us that you are God
and it is in worshipping you
and in following you that the real beauty of life is found.

Lead us not into temptation Lord, and deliver us from evil.

On giving things up for Lent

As a wise little six year old I asked my Great Aunt Aggie what she was going to give up for Lent. She was a tall woman with wire rimmed glasses, over which she would look at me from time to time. Dressed in black from head to foot, except on the Sabbath when she donned a large black hat, she was a caricature of the Victorian Scottish Presbyterian lady.
She peered down at me. "Colin," she spoke slowly, "if there is anything you need to give up for Lent, you should not be doing it anyway.

Lent 3 Debt Broken Jaw

When I saw 'John' for the first time he had his jaw wired up as the result of a fight in a pub car park during which he had been robbed of what little money he had left. Homeless, alcoholic, unwanted and heavily in debt, he was literally one step away from the street. Prison actually came as a blessing to him because in that month he cleared his Court fines, sobered up, had a chance to heal and gave us a chance to find him a bed and breakfast address on his release.

He could not understand why I was interested in helping him but he knew that without help and security he would soon be lost again. He joined Alcoholic's Anonymous and got himself a job as a cleaner in a new hotel. He also began to help in the bed and breakfast and he was soon allowed to act as the site manager.

The idea of owning his own place and running a bed and breakfast became something of an obsession with him and he saved all the money he might otherwise have spent on drink. So effective was this that he had the deposit for his first house before the year was out and his first tenant was admitted three months later.

John kept in touch with me voluntarily, often inviting me to see what he had done to the house, then to the opening of his second house. He only took referrals from us as a way of saying thanks for the way we had been there for him. He now sees his sons and is respected again by his family though he remains essentially a lonely man.

The last time I saw him he hooted at me and drove his car to the side of the road so that he could get out to greet me. As he drove off he smiled as he said "It's a long way from the broken jaw!"

Forgive us our debts so that we may repay you with love.

Lent 4 Mother God

Wonderful God, there are so many ways to describe the great things that you do for us.
We call you Father and mother, creator of the world.
True parent of us all.
We call you Son of God,
saviour of humankind
We call you Spirit alive in us today,
caring for us with a mother's love,
comforting us, feeding us, teaching us,
correcting us, believing in us,
preparing us to be your people in this world.

Now dear Lord we come to you as children
who have fallen yet again;
but our bumps and bruises are self inflicted sins,
the things that we know are wrong.
We still behave like disobedient children
leaving our toys scattered for others to pick up.
We wait until we think you are out of the room
before doing what you have just told us not to do,
and failing to do the things you want us to do.

How we depend on your never failing love and forgiveness.
Help us we pray to be like you
so that in all our roles in life,
child, brother, sister, friend, husband,
wife, father, mother, grandparent,
we may always try to live
with the love that you have shown us.

Passion Sunday Communion

Taste the bitter herbs of Passover
and eat to make us fit;
fit to travel across an unknown desert's sand;
fit to seek a promised land
where humankind and God shall fully live,
for God does love and does forgive
those who really share his feast.

Eat of the Christ bread,
for what we eat is broken heart and soul,
hung on a cross because of love's great need
to heal the sick, to help the hungry feed,
to free, give hope, to let all people live,
for God does love and does forgive
those who really share his feast.

Drink of the Christ wine,
for what we drink is blood and tear,
tears shed for those who die alone,
blood shed when people will not own
the life and hope he freely gives,
for God does love and does forgive
those who really share his feast.

Feed on the Christ food,
for what we taste is life in all its fullness,
life wholly given, life that is meant to share,
life spent and bent in service and in prayer,
life consumed in everything we give
to God, who loves and does forgive
those who really share his feast.

Palm Sunday **Why me?**

I don't know why you have chosen me
to be one of your friends. I'm no saint!
Yet you say you want me as I am,
with all my life experience
to love others, without exception,
as you have loved me.

Help me I pray,
especially when I am tempted
by the negative presumptions of my upbringing,
by the prejudice I have been taught,
by my natural desire to pass by evil quietly
and not to disturb it,
to pretend I have not seen,
nor heard the suffering of your world.

Why you have called me I do not know,
but you have raised me up
from service to friendship.
You have clasped my hand and made me welcome
in the house of God.

I do want to serve you and do what is right.
Take me and make me worthy of such trust,
so that those who meet me may also find you,
your love rejoicing in all I do,
your joy dancing through my faith,
your life offered in all its fullness through mine
then we may ride together into Jerusalem.

Good Friday **Simon of Cyrene**

The crowd was restless,
waiting,
murmuring to one another.
In the distance women were wailing.
A voice cried out, "He is coming".
Roman spears glinted
through a gap among the heads
and polished shields gleamed
in the morning sun.

"There he is!" a voice cried,
and the crowd began to shout abuse,
even those who knew it was a lie,
scared to say they knew him.
The soldiers headed in my way,
forcing the crowds aside
to jeer and jostle in their wake.
Suddenly they were in front of me
and he stumbled,
the rough wood splintering down his back,
raking into his previous wounds.
I stretched out my hand
but he fell, his body worldly weak.
The soldiers cursed him, lashed him,
hauled him to his broken feet,
then saw he could not bear the load.

They seized me and gave me the cross
to carry in his place
up to the hill's accursed crest.
Ahead of me he stumbled on,
each movement full of pain
at the venom of those
who scorned his battered frame,
mocking, swearing,
though some began to pray.

I walked as if trapped in a spell,
caught in a living nightmare,
a parody of myself,
both onlooker and participant.
On we climbed,
his shame becoming mine,
but as we reached our destination
I felt that he had known me all the time
and he had borne my burdens.

It was he who bore the deepest bruises,
the cruellest pain, and our betrayal
with the fondest of embraces
and the greatest love of all.

Saturday Nightmare

O GOD !
How terrible it is to think that you are dead!
All our hope and vision;
all the incentive to love instead of hate;
all the light of our life snuffed out.
When we look at the world without you
we are shocked by it's cruelty.
Even so we try - to love where there is rejection,
to make peace where there is conflict,
to bring hope to those who despair,
to heal where the world is wounded.
But we are bruised and beaten;
powerlessly we wait for death
and we watch those we love die without your comfort.
People blame us for being silent
and curse us when we speak.
Without you, nothing makes sense,
there is no reason to love,
no reason to hope, to live.
But you are God!
The desolate, the sinner, the grieving, the suffering, the poor,
The whole world needs you to make life meaningful,
worth while, forgiving, and accepting.
Only you can take away our fears by your love;
only you make sense of life.

It is easy to believe that Good Friday was the end;
but that is a nightmare.
It is today that God in Christ takes our place.

Today is the day he dies for us.
This is the day that the Lord has made.
Let us rejoice and be glad in it.

Easter Sunday

FOUR STEP

Love King tied down,
they mock, flog, nail.
Hang life on cross,
on dung heap hill.

Seal him in tomb
hard rock made door
Make sure this king
Lies dead, rock sure.

They wept for love,
alone with grief,
then life came back,
with new belief

From dead days rise,
to life anew,
know that love wins,
. God's word is true.

Christ is alive
The Spirit free
And still today
Christ lives for me.

Easter Monday **Be not afraid!**

Mary sat by the empty tomb weeping with sorrow. The other women had run away when they angel spoke to them because they were so scared. He had said *'Don't be afraid, we have good news for you'.*

The disciples were locked away in hiding because they were so scared when suddenly Jesus was there in the middle of them. *'Shalom'* he said, *'Don't be afraid, I have good news for you'*

Shepherds had once looked at the wonderful star that shone over Bethlehem and were also keeping an eye on the sheep when without warning a heavenly choir of angels burst into their peaceful life and scared the wits out of them!
'Don't be afraid we have come to bring you good news.'

If we think about it we would also have been very frightened by what was happening. After all we are rational human beings and things like that just don't happen to us. Do they?

The doctor came in to the room I was in. "Good news! You have T.B."
I was afraid. "Good news!!" I declared, "what's good about that?"

"It is good," he replied, "because now we know that you can live!"

Good news is not always what we want to or expect to hear but it is always an opportunity to be alive and to do so in a new and fuller way.

God calls us to be the bearers of his good news even though it may upset our ideas and change our expectations. It may well be shocking and frightening but at all times we have the promise,
'Do not be afraid because I am with you at all times.'

Easter 2 Thomas

It is Easter time again and once more we hear the amazing stories of
your triumphant entry into Jerusalem,
the tragedy of your betrayal and death,
and the incredible events of your resurrection.

I can't even pretend to understand what happened or how it happened and in some ways I would have been like Thomas,
wanting to believe but needing more that just a story.
Poor Thomas, he got more than he had bargained for.

Do you believe because you see me? How happy are those who believe without seeing me!

Yes Lord, I believe even though I do not know,
even though I have doubts about some of the stories.
I believe it happened and the evidence isn't just what happened to Jesus but in the whole resurrection of his followers and the whole illogical witness of millions of people ever since;
in spite of all the opposition,
in spite of the way we keep messing your church up,
in spite of our doubts, in spite of our sin.

I believe because everything we stand for makes sense in a senseless world.
Until we accept that, we will still crucify the innocent
by warfare, hunger, ignorance, hatred and by all the evil ways that enslave people and deny them the love of God.

Forgive them Father, they don't know what they are doing.
Lord forgive us because we do know what we are doing.

Easter 3 Fishermen

"Come" said Peter, "let's go fishing,
Let's go out upon the lake.
Better that than sit here wishing.
We are fishermen for goodness sake."

So off we sailed across the lake
and cast our nets over the side
but there was nothing for our efforts sake,
and all our labour was denied.

The nets were trailing on the side
as morning broke above the hill
and we were weary and denied,
our bodies tired, the water still

Then by the sunlight above the hill
we saw a figure on the shore.
He called across the waters still,
"Come fishermen, try just once more."

So who is this upon the shore
when we have struggled all the night
to tell us just to try once more?
"Cast out" he cried, "cast to the right".

Though we had struggled all the night,
he made us think of once before
and so we cast out to the right
and filled our nets up by the score.

Just as it had been once before
and John cried out "It is the Lord!
That's why we land fish by the score,
He promised us, he keeps his word."

When Peter saw it was the Lord
he stripped and dived into the lake
and swam to greet the promised word
by charcoal fire with fish to bake.

To shore we rowed across the lake
and with our Lord we broke some bread,
sat round the fire as fish was baked
and listened to each word he said.

We shared the fish and broke the bread
while he told us to keep on fishing,
but not like now is what he said.
"Seek you the lost, the poor, the wishing."

"Yes !" cried Peter, "We'll go fishing,
fishing in life's teeming lake,
seek the lost the poor, the wishing,
be fishermen for God's own sake."

Easter 4 With sadness

We remember with sadness the suffering of so many people,
Suffering caused by wars that can never be won
for they spawn the hatred and hurt of generations still to come.
Suffering caused by hunger and disease which could have been avoided.
Suffering caused by those who are blinded by bigotry, racial hatred, religious intolerance.

Lord what terrible things are done in your name.
Help us make your love for all people known,
Show us how to bring your peace,
how to give all your world hope for the future.

We remember with sadness the way in which your church has divided itself as if one gift was the only gift.
Help us build the bridges that will make us work together for your kingdom and not just for our own vision of that glory.

We remember with sadness when we have not loved
We pray for those with whom we are in any form of dispute.
Help us to forgive those who have hurt us
and to pray for those whose behaviour causes us distress.

We pray for those who have sought gods of their own destruction in drink, drugs, violence and hatred.
We pray for those who are suffering serious illness,
for those who are frightened of what is happening to them,
for those who need God's loving touch in their life,
especially those we know.
Finally Lord we pray for ourselves that you may take us
and help us to be the people you would like us to be.

Easter 5 — Hungry child

Why little child? Why do you weep?
In all your tender years
those eyes have had no peaceful sleep.
They weep but have no tears.

You sit there on the scorching earth,
beneath a cloudless sky,
as children did before your birth
and they too could not cry.

The sun beats down upon your frame,
there is no shady home.
Nobody seems to know your name,
and nobody bids you come.

Those eyes reflect a million prayers.
Give me my daily bread.
Give me some water for my tears
and life before I'm dead.

Easter 5 is often close to Christian Aid Week

Easter 6 Friends

You have raised us up to be your friends Lord.
Though we were strangers to you and even enemies,
you have made us your friends,
yet we continue to behave like children
who are always falling out with each other over the smallest thing,
especially when we don't get our own way.,
always wanting you to do what we want;
wanting you to be like us.

Forgive us we pray and still be our friend,
for when we are without you it is as if we are lost.
We still do the same things but life has no meaning.
Forgive us for we are always asking you to do things for us
always looking for our peace, our joy,
our sense of being loved.
We want to be treated with justice,
to have hope in our lives,
to be well fed and healthy
but we do not do our best
to provide the same for the rest of your children.
We turn off the television if it causes us pain or unease,
We stop caring about your world
and pretend it is nothing to do with us
or that we can't do anything.

Lord you are a friend to all those who we reject or fear.
You tell us the truth because you are our friend,
and we try not to hear you,
You show us the way but we chose the easy directions,
You show us life in all its fullness
yet we stick to our own little version.
Forgive us and help us to be the friends you would like us to be

Easter 7 **When God says No**

Help us we pray to understand when you say no Lord
and forgive us for the anger and upset we feel
when we don't get what we wanted.

Forgive us for the way we sulk
when we don't get our own way.

Forgive us we pray for we are always rejecting you
in the ways we live our life, the life that you have given us.
We do things that we know would displease you.
We fail to do what would please you.
We seek our rewards in this life
and make our judgements based on our success or failure.

Help us we pray to see beyond our own feelings
to the glory of your kingdom.
Help us to be the people who are your ministers,
who live lives that speak of you,
who don't let our distress blind us to your great love,
to that love which is so great that Jesus was willing to die for us.

When we feel downcast Lord, pick us up,
dust us down and point us in the way to go.
We are your people, weak and sinful though we are,
help us be the best we can,
in your everlasting love, your strength, in your way..

Ascension **Coming down the mountain**

Suddenly the teacher is gone. Christ has returned to the Father; Jesus the Son of Man is glorified in the heavens, and we must get ready for his Spirit is to come upon us,

Lord, fill us with the joy of your disciples coming down from the mountain.

> Share with us the glory of the ascended Christ
> and prepare us to receive the gift of the Holy Spirit
> so that we too may be your witnesses of salvation.

We would be your people of faith and love.
Teach us the wisdom that reveals your justice and peace;
open our minds to see and to show the light of your forgiveness;
inspire us to rejoice in the hope to which you call your children;
give us a sense of the great richness of the life you promise,
and bless us with your wonderful power.

> The power that raised Christ from death,
> and seats him at God's side in heaven
> from where he rules over all the nations
> all time and all creation.

Lord, fill us with the joy of your disciples coming down from the mountain.

> Share with us the glory of the ascended Christ
> and prepare us to receive the gift of the Holy Spirit
> so that we may be your witnesses of salvation

Pentecost **Wake up Christian**

Wake up, Christian! for there's a real world waiting,
waiting for a reconciling Christ.
A world that is weeping ,
with danger, fear and passion,
teeming with disordered, joyless life.

Wake up, Christian! for there's a real child screaming,
screaming in the hurt of shattered lives;
an ache that is gnawing,
of anger, guilt and sorrow,
yearning for a loving, healing Christ.

Wake up, Christian! for there's a real hate burning,
burning in each prejudicial pain.
A hate that is frightening,
denying and destroying,
hanging Christ upon the cross again.

Wake up, Christian! for there's a real void yawning,
yawning in the people without faith.
There is no believing
in gospel, hope and worship,
souls are trapped in lives that waste away.

Wake up, Christian! for there's a real Christ with you,
with you as you travel on your way.
A Christ who is loving ,
challenging, forgiving,
living through you this and every day.

Trinity Travellers

We are travelling companions on the pilgrimage of life,
though we walk our different passages we can journey in the light
of the God who in his joyfulness created all the world,
and made us in his image by the breathing of a word.

Many find the journey is a long and painful trail,
and fear can make them flounder in the dark so they never find the way,
but with love and hope and gentleness we can guide them through the night,
by a step into their darkness and the sharing of our light.

There are those who build up barriers and foster war and hate,
For their goal is power and privilege and they never want to wait,
but the torch we bear is peacefulness and its beam reveals their wrong
by showing ways of justice for those who limp along.

God has given all his children hearts to show his rainbow love
and he calls on us to share our life while he keeps us on the move,
for our souls are full of restlessness until the day is come
when all the world can see the light and travel safely home.

Though we walk by tempting alleys that could make us go astray,
the road is lit ahead of us by the glory Christ displays
and in all our times of helplessness he is there to lift our load,
for the God who made the heavens walks beside us on the road

Pentecost 2 **Preacher's Prayer**

Give me a voice Lord!
A voice that will proclaim
the wonder of your love to me,
and out aloud declare your fame.
A voice that will not mumble
but clearly states your name.

Give me a voice Lord
that will not fade away,
in youth or age or cowardice.
Remove the fears that make me stay
my talk of your great loving,
my loving what you say.

Give me a voice Lord
to set trapped spirits free.
A voice that will announce the news
that debts are paid and we can be
released from blinkered vision,
forgiven, healed and clean.

Give me a voice Lord
so others may find voice
to challenge the unrighteous deed,
to help the poor and weak rejoice,
be comfort to the dying,
and give your world a choice.

Pentecost 3 That's not me!!

Alice came from a good family, a professional family and a family destroyed by alcohol. Her father had committed suicide; her mother had been in hospital and her brother had been killed in a car crash. She had turned more and more to her boy friend and to the drugs that were easily available within the clubs and parties they frequented. Drugs helped her forget her grief and they kept her away from drinking.

By the time I met her she was injecting heroin and she was rarely able to work. She still had the security of home but this was also the centre point of her sadness.

Being arrested and put on probation was a shock to Alice. She didn't want to accept she had a problem even when she became seriously ill and nearly died. That did however make her value life and so we began to work on her motivation. The drugs however still had hold of her until one day when she was visiting the hospital. She needed a fix so she nipped into the ladies.

As she was about to inject herself she saw a sign on the door "Drug Addicts. Please do not use this cubicle to fix in as it may be used by children." She had stopped and thought "Who in their right mind would do that?" Then she realised that it was her. She told me later that she had cried for about ten minutes trying to say "It's not me! It's not me!"

We began to work on a social functioning questionnaire after that to see if it could give her a lead. One of the questions asked her to say how far she had achieved her ambition in life. Her nought had scared her because she had no idea of ambition beyond the next fix. I asked her to think about that question before our next meeting and to think what she wanted, even if it seemed impossible.

The following week she returned and she knew what she wanted to do. It was to be a nurse working with alcoholics and drug addicts. She had said this before to people but it had always been dismissed as impossible. We began to look at what would make it possible.

For the next year Alice stayed at a clinic clearing her system of the poison of the drugs. It was hard and at times very frightening for her. Several times she nearly gave up. Then the day came when she came home. Target two was about to begin.

At least twelve months in a job without relapse. At the end of that year she was accepted for training and when I last heard from her she had become a sister on a ward dealing with addictions. She still had to fight her own addictive nature but her determination was heart warming to see. The last I heard of her was on a television programme on which she was speaking about a new centre for the treatment of addictions.

Pray for those who need something to make life worthwhile, a vision of the future even if the odds seem great. Pray that those who are trapped by addiction may find a way to change and to become the people that God would like them to be.

Pentecost 4 **Refugee** (based on a true story)

How can I tell you my name?
I who have seen
my fellow man in his deepest shame.
I who can tell you of his obscenities,
for I have seen him in the night
come to murder and destroy
all that was precious in my sight,
all that gave my family joy.
And why? What did we do?
We did not rise up against their rule;
we only spoke of what was true
and would not countenance the cruel.
But when corruption wears the crown
then those who dare to say "This is not right"
become a danger to be put down.

So Christians vanish in the night,
for evil cannot face the day,
nor wickedness be seen for what it does.
We all lived in fear and some chose to obey
the orders that deprave the soul.
We cried for justice, but their violation
of our lives is unseen by the law,
for it must serve the rulers of the nation
and all that we have seen it never saw.
No one from my old school now lives at home
and only ten from eighty two survive
as rootless, nationless we roam,
thankful to God that we were kept alive.

Yet guilty too, and sleepless still
for our eyes always scour the night
because we are the witnesses they failed to kill,
our tongues can speak, our eyes have sight.
So I live here, a refugee,
not from a famine, war nor flood,
but for my faith, my Christianity,
for doing what I knew was good.
Even so I fight my human nature,
holding to grace and life as it should be,
and stifling the angry vengeful creature
that roars within the very heart of me.

Only by the power of faith in a crucified and tortured Lord
can I share in the love that conquers death
and understand how hope springs from his blood.
Such is this gift of love
that Presidents must tremble, evil be confused
for life does rise, and rise again to prove
that truth and hope survive however badly used.

And I forgive,
my brothers did not know
except that they too wanted to survive
and chose that way to follow.
And I forgive,
or else I shall be murdered by their shame.
The memory of their deeds will live.
I do not need to speak my name.

Pentecost 5 Giants

I have been reading the story of Jesus calming the storm and discovered that far from being safe they were blown ashore on Gadara, the most unholy place imaginable.
Suddenly they were faced with the giant Mob charging at them from the grave stones, his chains swirling above his head.
I can just see your disciples Lord,
Scrambling to get back to sea and escape from this monster;
but you stood your ground and he was turned from his madness
into your disciple, a witness to your love.

Forgive us Lord! We are such easily frightened people.
Anyone who is different or challenging makes us stand back.
Those who are violent and criminal, drugged or drunk,
those whose behaviour is irrational,
those who destroy ......and kill!
Lord ! Do you really expect us to love them as well?

Help us we pray, to love as you have loved:
to challenge evil wherever it is,
but to see with your eyes the soul that cries out in its pain,
the person within the terrible deed.

Teach us to stand fast for your love;
to make peace where there is torment,
to bring forgiveness where we are deeply hurt,
to heal where there is deep wounding,.
to bring hope where all hope seems lost.
Everybody is invited to your party
and you have called us to make sure
that they all get an invitation,
even the scary ones.

Pentecost 6 Comfort zone

Wonderful God, it is good to be here again to worship you
for this is a place where we can really show you how much we love
you by singing and praying and learning more
about your wonderful world.
Here we can give you thanks for Jesus and praise you for his life
and for the way in which you sent him into this world
to share our life
Here we can rejoice in the presence of the Holy Spirit,
the very essence of God with us now.
God has given us peaceful hearts and kindly natures.
Here we are comfortable.

Father forgive us for staying where we feel safe and content.
for choosing friends who will only agree with us
for letting the things we have
become more important than you.
for not caring about others and being self centred
for turning away from people because they are not like us
for not having enough faith in you to do new things.

Lord, help us to be brave enough
to move out of our comfort zones
and to be the people you would like us to be,
people who are willing to go where you would go,
to do what you would do, to care as you would care,
to show our love by the way we praise you
to show your love by the way we serve you
and live our lives
in the name of Jesus Christ.

Pentecost 7 Who is my neighbour?

The school was closed for the tatty holidays in October, when the whole village spent two weeks bent double to get the potato crops in. Being only seven was no excuse for we were still at war and there were few men around. At first light a lorry trundled down the street collecting all the howkers, as the workers were known.

As we arrived the bits were marked out. These were the area for you to pick as the digger churned past and threw up the crop. I had a half bit but it still seemed a very long way to go dragging a creel (wire basket) behind me for the muddy potatoes to be thrown in.

The farmer was an elderly man with few words and only one adjective.
Both I and my mother began to flag at the unusual exercise. The young man driving round to collect the potatoes in a lorry stopped and jumped down to help us. "Here" he said, "it will be easier if you do it this way."

Each day he would do the same, not just for us but all round the field. I think he must have picked half the potatoes himself in spite of the shouting of the farmer who was sitting on a chair at the other side of the field smoking a pipe.

We saw him in the barn when we stopped for lunch on the first day and thanked him for his help. He smiled and said "It was my pleasure." Then he went and sat with the tractor driver. My mother leant over and said quietly, "They are Germans Colin. Prisoners of War at the camp in Belmont."

I looked at them wondering why they didn't seem to be different from us like the paper said. All my knowledge of Germans was from the radio the Dundee Courier and the Saturday Daily Express. We could only afford one copy a week of each and that was mainly to recycle in the toilet.

Over the week we discovered that his name was Richard and that he came from Cologne. He had been just sixteen when the whole class was conscripted, and seventeen when he was shot in the leg and captured. The next weekend we heard of how we had bombed Cologne. It didn't seem such a victorious thing when we saw Richard weeping in the corner of the barn. Even so he continued to help as usual and to talk to me when he stopped nearby.

After the harvest my mother kept contact with Richard and he was allowed to visit us for two hours at Christmas. He was so unlike any other man that I knew with his kindness. My great aunt with whom we lived at that time had a harmonium and she played some carols while he was there. I remember especially him singing 'Stillen Nacht'.

We moved to London soon afterwards and the war ended. By the time we returned to Ardler he had been repatriated. I still remember him every time I hear that carol, my enemy, my friend, my neighbour.

God make us friends who once were strangers,
Break down the barriers of sin.
Teach us how we may walk together
So life is shared and love begins. *(Sharing Jesus 2009)*

Pentecost 8 **Words**

Lord God, we love the gifts you have given us
but sometimes we don't use them
in the way you meant us to.
Today we think of the gift of words
and of your wisdom.
our ability to talk and to listen and to learn.

How often we forget to listen,
to wait for your word,
to let others speak so that we might share
their worries,
their joys,
their fears
and sadness.

Lord forgive us and give us the grace to listen
so that we might hear.

How often we chatter away,
speaking a lot and saying very little,
being careless of what others would like to say,
being full of our own opinions,
caring little about what we say.

Lord forgive us and give us the grace
to be aware of the need of others.

How often we stay silent when we should speak,
silent when others speak harmfully,
silent when your name is taken in vain,
silent when your love is needed in someone else's life.

Lord forgive us and give us
the grace to know when we should speak and what we can say.

There are times Lord when we have taken
the words of your Bible
and used them out of context
to make them sound as if they agree with us,
and not with those who disagree with us.
Forgive us we pray,
help us to cherish your Bible and to use it wisely

How often have our words been careless
and sometimes hurtful,
words used in anger,
words used to control and demean,
words used spitefully.

Lord forgive us and give us the grace to think before we speak.

How often have we not spoken to you Lord,
or given ourselves a chance to listen
to what you might want to say to us.

Lord forgive us and give us
the grace to pray so that we may be at peace with you
and with our neighbours wherever and whoever they might be.

Speak to us Lord that we may speak wisely
the words that you want us to say.

Pentecost 9 **Martha dear Martha**

Martha, dear Martha, the salt of the earth,
I know that you love me, I know of your worth;
but what are you missing as you tidy and clean?
The room will need dusting long after I'm gone.

Martha, dear Martha, your cooking is great,
your jams and preserves grace every church fete
but what are you missing by cooking a cake?
There will be plenty of eating long after I'm gone.

Martha, dear Martha, the rooms are all fine
and I shall sleep well on the mat that is mine,
but what are you missing with all of your fuss?
There is plenty of worry long after I'm gone.

Martha, dear Martha, your work speaks for you
and everyone knows you are faithful and true
but what are you missing in all of your chores?
There is plenty of service long after I'm gone.

Come sit with your sister and share in our chatter.
I love you as well. It's this time that matters.
For what you are missing with all that is done
is the time to be with me before I am gone.

Pentecost 10 Treasures

It's the moments when we realise
the closeness of God's presence,
the cool oasis, quiet place,
the loving hug and friendly face,
these are the times we treasure.

Good friends who listen patiently
when trouble seeks compassion,
where love can share a healing space
and condemnation has no place,
these are the folk we treasure.

For love which holds us when we fail
and stands by us in weakness,
where sadness finds a safe embrace
and tears are wiped from sorrow's face,
these are the deeds we treasure.

Where in a fellowship of faith
we find a true devotion,
where people work to show God's grace
and share his feast in holy place,
this is the church we treasure.

Pentecost 11 Finding God

Is this where you can be found Lord?
High up in the billowing cloud
using it as Blake portrayed
to cover you like a shroud,
until some whim should stir you
to rend the clouds asunder
and reach down in a lightning flash
to speak amidst the thunder.

Is this where you can be found Lord?
Deep in the volcano's heart,
seeking appeasement from your people,
pouring out your molten soul to part
the seas upon the steaming shore
with nothing but destruction left upon your path,
and those who worship bowing down
before your awesome wrath.

Is this where you can be found Lord?
On the depths of the ocean bed,
with the waters of creation
waving ceaselessly above your head.
Are you he who formed the land
out of rock and coral reef?
Are you planning for our future,
beyond our disbelief?

Is this where you can be found Lord?
In the wilderness of my soul,
waiting for my awakening
so that you can make me whole.
Did you breathe your breath into me
and in your image make
the people of this planet
as friends for loves own sake?

Is this where you can be found Lord?
In the worship that I give,
by my care of your creation
and love in the way I live.
Then the clouds and fiery mountain
the seas and all the lands
will share with humankind in praise
to God who understands.

Pentecost 12 Kingdom come

Loving God, we pray that your Kingdom may come,
that it may come in the places of conflict
where people so desperately need to know your peace,
and to learn how to forgive each other
for the terrible damage of warfare, hatred and abuse of power.
Let your will be done

Through our lives and by our prayers, your Kingdom come

Loving God, we pray that your Kingdom may come,
that it may come in places of great need,
where people die because of hunger, or polluted water,
where they live impoverished lives
because of ignorance and lack of ability to care for themselves,
where they have no place to live,
no power to change by themselves.
Let your will be done

Through our lives and by our prayers, your Kingdom come

Loving God, we pray that your Kingdom may come,
that it may come where people have wealth and power,
for those in government that they may do so justly and honourably,
for those whose talent and ability influences the young,
that they may remember that all their gifts are God-given.
Let your will be done.

Through our lives and by our prayers, your Kingdom come

Loving God we pray that your Kingdom may come
that it may come in your church,
so that in a society where so many people
do not think you are important
we have the determination to make sure your message is heard.
We pray for your churches here in this town
and give thanks for the ministry of all those who proclaim your word
and ensure the continuation of your gospel.
Let your will be done.

Through our lives and by our prayers, your Kingdom come

Loving God, we pray that your Kingdom may come,
that it may come where people are suffering from grave illness,
where they weep from sadness, are disabled by depression,
where they are weak and weary.
For those we know who need your loving touch at this time we pray
Pause for private prayer.
Lord hear our prayer and let your will be done

Through our lives and by our prayers, your Kingdom come.

Loving God we pray that your Kingdom may come,
that it may come in each of us so that when life is difficult we may face our troubles knowing that your love is there to sustain and comfort us, and that when we are challenged by your Spirit we may not shrink from your call but embrace it with all our faith and respond with as much love as you have shown us.
Let your will be done

Through our lives and by our prayers, your Kingdom come.

entecost 13 Taken for granted

With all the wonder of what God has done for us
how can we take it for granted,
as if it isn't important to our everyday life?
But we do and so we must confess Lord,
that we are not the people you would like us to be.

We cling to our own comfort in a world of suffering and need.
We hold opinions that condemn others
when we do not know or understand them
and worst of all just because they are different
We seek popularity instead of justice or truth
and are afraid of speaking about God's love
outside the safety of the church.
We shut our eyes when we are challenged
by the sadness of those around us
We turn to you when it suits us
and expect you to be there when we are in need.

Forgive us we pray and give us an active passion about your uncomfortable world.
Give us the grace to welcome all your people,
the faith that has no fear of the future,
and the compassion that thinks of others
and not just of ourselves.
Forgive us when we fall short
of the opportunities you give us,
and fail to appreciate the life you have given us.
Bless us so that we never forget what you have done.
Or dare to take it for granted.

Pentecost 14 City church

From riverside to railway, from factory to hotel,
from humble terraced houses and shops that buy and sell,
in hoots of car and riverboat,
in all the voices stirred
among the great cacophony,
the voice of God is heard.

Here still the faithful gather to worship, serve and pray,
to be the face of Jesus within his world today.
Though ageing and uncertain,
Their numbers getting less,
they spend their little energy
and try to do their best.

The buildings are now crumbling, they have more faith than cash,
yet they still have a vision,
though others call it rash,
for here within this island of river road and rail,
they know that hope is needed
and love can still prevail.

Their faith is like a fortress against the world's decay,
for God is just as relevant as he was yesterday,
and so his healing, peace and joy,
his wine and bread are shared.
In all their loving witness
God's mercy is declared

Pentecost 15 Freedom

Suffering God, we come to praise you
as free men and women,
able to enjoy health care, work, education,
wealth and the opportunity to work.
We pray for those who cannot share
the goodness of life with which you have blessed us.

Forgiving God, we come to praise you
as free men and women,
sustained and blessed by your Holy Spirit,
yet always surprised by the Spirit's challenge
to do your will and to take your love and forgiveness
into the dark places of life,
places where people find it difficult to know you
or to believe that you want to know then.

Forgive us we pray when we fail to recognise you in this wonderful world or to praise you for the gifts you have given us.
Forgive us when we turn our backs on those who suffer,
for when we take your goodness for granted,
for when we complain;
for when we are too comfortable to do your work in the world.

Forgive us when we deny your Spirit of change and opportunity,
when we shy away from those
who seek our care, our love, our help.
Forgive us for the slavery that continues even today
and in this land.

Help us, we pray, to stand for your justice
and the freedom of all people in the name of Jesus Christ

Harvest **Sow me**

Sow me in the desert sands,
sow me on rock and stony ground,
sow me in the thistle and the thorn,
for only when you sow me can I make the desert bloom,
turn thorns into a holy crown and rocks into a tomb.

Sow me in the market places,
sow me in the hard and mocking hearts,
sow me in the prison and the pub;
for only when you sow me can I make my loving real,
bring peace instead of anger and hope instead of fear.

Sow me in the darkest night,
sow me in death and helpless tears,
sow me in the sickness and the pain;
for only when you sow me can I bring a healing light,
release the grieving spirit or give the blinded sight.

Sow me in your work and prayer,
sow me in all the ways you take,
sow me in the people that you meet.
I need you to sow me whatever is around,
for anyone can sow me on good and fertile ground.

Pentecost 16 Peace Prayer

Dear God, we ask your forgiveness
for our rejection of you today,
for the warring nature of nations, tribes and even ourselves.
For our unwillingness to listen to other views,
other ideas, other ages, colours, gender.
We are always disagreeing with each other
and behaving with suspicion and distrust.
Yet you left us with your great gift of love and peace,
with your Shalom.

Lord we weep for the past,
for the folly of wars that destroyed families, cities, nations,
forgive us for the hatred which remains from the past.
We weep for today, for the wars which cannot be won,
for the extremism of radical religiosity,
for the thought that one ideal should be imposed on others,
for the idea that winning is justification for murder,
that terror can be acceptable.
Lord we are still in great need of your forgiveness
and understanding of peace.

We weep for the homes in which conflict is a way of life.
Where children grow up in an abusive relationship,
where one person thinks that they can own or dominate another.
Where people say they hate each other.

Forgive us for being afraid to speak out about God's love for everyone,
for failing to see the hope that God has for us all.
Forgive us for failing to forgive,
and for being your Shalom.

Pentecost 17 Regrets

Lord, we have so many things for which to be grateful
that we should live constantly in the glory of your grace.
Sadly we fail to do so
and as such we are always coming back to you with our apologies.
Sorry Lord!
It is so easy to forget in our every day life that you are there with us.

Forgive us we pray
for the times we have acted without love,
for the selfishness that denies our love,
for the hasty words,
for our rejection of others
for the times we have done things you would not want us to do;
for the times we have failed to do what we ought to have done;
for the people we do not like;
for arguments and all acts that separate us
from each other and from you.

Take all that we have offered here,
our sadness, sorrow and regrets,
judge each of us as we deserve,
for it is in the love of Christ that we find our salvation,
it is in your grace and mercy that we find forgiveness.

On that love, grace and mercy Lord we depend.

Pentecost 18 Blind abseiling

The voice said come,
and though I could not see
through the darkness,
I knew I must believe.
So I moved towards the voice,
gently feeling the way,
trusting in what he would tell me.

The voice said 'jump',
trust in me to hold you,
you will not fall.
I knew I must believe,
so I jumped at his command,
letting myself go,
trusting in what he had told me.

The voice said 'love',
and held me until I was safe,
guiding me to the light.
I do believe that in my heights
and depths and darkness,
all things can be done,
trusting in God's guidance.

Pentecost 19 Crumbs of comfort

(Luke 16 vs. 19-31) *I suppose Lord, that the rich man believed that Lazarus was responsible for his own condition. He probably thought that he was being kind in letting Lazarus wait with the dogs for the bread on which he wiped his hands. After all it was none of his business - was it?*

Forgive us Lord for the crumbs of comfort
that we offer to your starving world.
Forgive us for the self indulgence
which is blind to the suffering of your children.
Forgive us for letting wealth and the desire to get rich
lead us into foolish and harmful behaviour.
Forgive us for thinking that one big win
will sort out all our problems.
When we are blessed with worldly attributes,
keep us from showing off,
or thinking that we have achieved anything
that you have not given us.

Teach us we pray, to hope in the certainty of your love,
    to use our wealth wisely and justly,
    to be rich in good works,
    to be generous and ready to share,
    to value the lives of those about us
    and never give in to greed, envy, or pride.
For you are our God,
from whom all life springs and to whom all life returns.
You are our wealth, the harvest of our labours,
bread for the hungry, sight for the blind,
freedom for the oppressed, hope for the desperate,
home for the homeless, safety for the refugee,
and judge of how we live your life.

Pentecost 20 One World

Great God, your love has called us here.
The love which saw this whole world
and all of humankind created
to be your friends and companions to each other;

The love which saw your only son Jesus Christ
come to share this life with us
and to suffer as we suffer, to die as we die,
but then to rise from our death to your eternal life
so that we might be put right with you.

The love which moves among us now
as the Holy Spirit shares our everyday,
comforting, challenging,
being with each of us in our time of need,
hearing our prayers and giving us strength to do God's will.

Almighty God we do not live up to your hope for us
and we are always in need of you gently redirecting us
and forgiving us.
Today we remember we are part of the one world
that you created,
part of the rich variety of people
with whom you call us to share the riches of this world.

But we do not remember this all the time and we seek only the best
for ourselves regardless of the cost to others.
Forgive us we pray

We live in a world of rich and poor,
but your love for us all is the same.
We live in a world of power and powerlessness,
but your love for us all is the same.
We live in a world where children starve to death,
while we complain about our weight,
but your love for us all is the same.
We plunder your earth's resources
without regard for its effect on the world
just to feed our comfort and easy life,
but your creation is for everyone.
We enslave nations with debt
and make it impossible for them to be free,
then when the poor come here to share our wealth
we deny them, insult them, imprison them,
but your love is for everybody.

Forgive us for our selfish and thoughtless way of life.
Forgive our careless use of your creation
Forgive us we pray for our lack of care.

Help us dear God to overcome our fear of others
and learn how we can best care for your world
and all its people
and share your gifts and love with everyone
in the best way we can
In the name of Jesus Christ who lived for us all.

Pentecost 21 Potatoes

Ken was released from Borstal early because they could not control him. He had a string of violent offences behind him and he had already told the Borstal welfare officer what he could do with the license I had to supervise.

I was therefore slightly surprised when he reported. I decided that I would accept his opinion about license and so I laid down the minimum that he had to conform to and promised that I would not expect any more than that unless he asked me.

I then said, and why I did I cannot remember, "But if I were you, I would want to know how I can turn all that anger into something positive so that it helps me rather than hurting others and destroying my life."

He looked at me as if I was crazy but he asked the question. "What do you mean?"

Over the next few months Ken's life began to stabilise. He found a job that used up a lot of his energy in a green grocers and he joined a local rugby team. That didn't last very long but at least it gave him the idea that the anger that burned inside him might have a way of being safely contained.

By being able to talk about his anger and to share the violence and abuse he had suffered as a child without being judged or threatened with punishment for what was ingrained in him he slowly began to feel in control of his life. When he found Heather it was like he had suddenly been forgiven. Life had meaning.

Ken kept in touch with me after his license was finished. He became manager of the shops and his boss effectively treated him as his own son. The anger was still there and did flare up from time to time but now that he was aware of it and how it could affect him he had developed his own little strategies for dealing with it. In the last letter I received from Ken he added a post script, "p.s. When it gets too much for me now, I take it out on the potatoes, love, Ken. "

Too often we are scared away by people's anger, failing to see the hurt person inside the violence. By recognising him as someone who could accept that anger and use it, instead of denying it and punishing him for it, Ken became the hard working, loving father and husband even though he still needed the potatoes.

Too often we shun people who frighten us. You cannot stop anger. It is an emotion we all have. When it dominates our behaviour it scares everyone including the individual concerned, but it is also a force for change and good. We seek the good life that is in us all.

Pray for those whose anger makes them rejected because of its negativity and destructiveness. Help them to see how the energy they have can be turned to good use.

Pentecost 22 All Saints

Even as we praise your name Lord,
even as we come to worship you,
we hold our hands up and confess to you
that we have not been the people that you would like us to be.

We have allowed the world's pressures to weigh too heavily on us.
We have allowed the world's pleasures to tempt us too much,
and as such we have put the world before you
and we have done things we should not have done
and failed to do what you would have wanted us to do.

In our comfort Lord we have become complacent
and we have taken your love for granted.
Lord forgive our selfishness and laziness.

Forgive the easy acceptance of the violence we see each day on our televisions.
Forgive us for being too busy to read your gospel,
or to be the people you would like us to be.

Help us to be thankful for all the little saints
who have guided us to this day
and in that thankfulness to be forgiving and generous
in both thought and deed.
Help us to be grateful and joyful at what you have done for us
and not to be afraid of showing our love for you
by loving the people with whom we share each day.

Think of the little saints who have helped you along your way. People who may never know what they did because they did it out of their love of God. As a child in the village of Ardler Bella was one of my little saints.

Bella

Bella told our fortune in the tea cups,
taught in the Sunday school
and served the meals on weekdays.
Bouquets made from buttercups and daisies
helped to make young bruises heal, dried tears,
brought smiles and made her young friends feel
that life was kind.
In war few words were said.
Her grief was quiet when her man was dead.
She soldiered on and never showed her cares
and we became the children loved instead
of those which she had once hoped would be theirs.

Pentecost 23 **Christian foolishness**

However much I try to avoid things that will make me look or feel foolish I seem to have a knack of failing quite abysmally at times. From the days when my mother put me into a Highland Dancing class I have had moments of forgetting my left and my right. It was the night of the exhibition that I embarked on my career of unintentional folly. At the end of the line I leapt to my right while the rest of the line leapt left towards me and so the Highland Laddy descended into chaos! It is the only time I was expelled!!

Sadly we all seem to live in fear of looking silly and therefore shy away from the unfamiliar task especially if it is centre stage. How actors must dread the potential out-take been seen again and again. I must confess a degree of fondness for those whose humanity leads them into mistakes. It makes me feel more normal. On the other hand perfection scares the wits out of me because it is a measure to which I cannot aspire.

God, however, does not measure us by our success or our failure but by our willingness to respond to his love. His mercy *'is not the results of your own efforts, but God's gift so that nobody can boast about it.'*

Being afraid is a normal response to things that are different or challenging, but if God's word is to be believed, which it should be by us then we do not need to let that fear stop us from being willing to risk being a fool for Christ. By faith we can do what God calls us to do. It is only by that faith that I dare to preach or write. If I jump the wrong way and nobody else is hurt, it is not the end of the world, indeed it is almost certainly worth a good laugh.

Pentecost 24 Cenotaph

Silence!
for those who stand to remember
among the grey and drizzle-sodden stone.
Chill November day for long lost loves
in faded pictures.
Stand still you aging bones and aching muscles.

Silence !
Booms the cannon,
two minutes for the dead we sent to die,
for the fearful and the brave
whose lives were mingled in the mud.
Comrades who laughed and cried and sang together.

Silence!
The shrill whistling starlings,
strutting their winter roosting ledges
have no thought for our yesterdays
nor for our poppy-flowered promises
and the silent walking of lost ways.

Silence!
They still go out to die in their obedience
and prayers for peace lack substance
when the dead might be our children.
The sacrifice of love still seeks
remembrance as our sign of sorrow.

Pentecost 25 Caged Earth

I saw a new Heaven and a new earth'
but it was a distant city -
Not so, says God.
You have been there since your birth
and I see you in its beauty.

But I can see great barriers and chains
holding me back from getting there -
Not so, says God.
You forge them from your fears and pains
to stop me getting in to share.

But I am weak and need to be protected
I cannot live without my safety line -
Not so, says God.
That city is your faith reflected
from here on earth and made divine.

But following you puts me in danger
and others will be different from me-
Not so, says God.
You make yourself the unknown stranger
and set your world within, instead of loving me.

But – Not so, says God.
It is you that makes the final choice
to greet the babe of Bethlehem
and only you can smash the cage
to let the Earth rejoice
and make of this world and today
the New Jerusalem.

Pentecost 26 Doing my best

I sometimes used to feel very inadequate Lord !
There were so many things that needed to be done
but I struggled to do them.
I looked at others and they seemed to manage so much better than I could.
Even at school I was keen but not as able as others.
They were cleverer, faster, stronger, they had lots of friends.

I felt sorry for the person who only had one talent.
I understood him.
It didn't matter what he did the others did it better.
And then I suddenly realised what it was that he did wrong.
He gave up!
Instead of doing what he could to the best of his ability,
he stopped bothering and did nothing.
He saw life as being a competition with others
and because he could not win he stopped competing.
But the competition is within.
It is the will to improve, to live life to the full,
to love and be loved for who and what you are
and to use your talent as an offering to God.

So Lord I offer all you have given me back to you by the way in which I live my life,
how I meet the challenges you give me day by day,
how I no longer fear being wrong or losing,
because this is the life you have given me
and in your grace and power
I shall be rich in Spirit and strong in love.
When you come to me I shall return your talent
with the best interest in life that I have been able to give it.

Pentecost 27 Patience

Fred was on probation for two years and I saw him and visited his family quite regularly over that time. The family was living in a tower block in South London and there was just Fred and his older sister. He was in his last year at school and it was clear that academic achievement was not his forte. In fact he had no great interest, no great ability and worst of all for me was that he was completely monosyllabic. In two years I don't think I ever heard him say more than yes or no, but he did keep out of any further trouble. His order finished 'satisfactorily' and I never expected to see him again.

Two years later I was told that Fred was waiting to see me. The change was almost unbelievable. He was bright eyed, keen and full of the fact that he had just passed his driving test (which was more than I had done at that time). We talked for half an hour about his great sense of achievement and how this had opened up new opportunities for work. Suddenly Fred believed in himself and in the future. He came to tell me before he had even been home.

I learned from Fred that being patient and accepting him as he was made me the only person who had not told him he was stupid and no good for anything. Although he had never said anything he had always reported on time and his meetings had meant so much more to him than I had ever credited. It was a privilege to share his joy and his success.

Pentecost 28 Rainbow and the Berlin Wall

I keep a rainbow in my Bible,
its seven twisted strands of wool,
knotted at either end,
was given to me with a prayer in the Summer of 1987.
May the wall between us be no more.
The wall is gone, the promise is alive.

I keep the rainbow in my Bible
to mark the gospel for the week;
this is the good news,
that what you ask for in his name
is not impossible and walls can tumble down,
this year, next year; in God's time.
The rainbow is still there, the promise is alive.

Healing Service Stand up

The story of Jairus and Veronica

This dramatised reading is based on the stories as told in Matthew 9 vs. 18-26, Mark 5 vs. 21-43 and Luke 8 vs. 40-56.
It has been used as part of a service and includes breaks for a hymn or a prayer. The intention is to show how both Jairus and Veronica (as other writings name her) had great obstacles to overcome before they came to Jesus, one because she was regarded as unclean and not allowed to mix with company and the other because he was too powerful and dared not be associated with Jesus. Healing goes beyond the physical.

Jairus My name is Jairus and I am the President of the Elders in the Synagogue. It is my job to see that all the worship in the Synagogue is right and according to the Law. Part of my work is to make sure that the Law of Moses is upheld at all times in the town as well as in the Synagogue.
I have been warned about the teachings of this man Jesus and I have listened carefully to what he says but it isn't just what he says that is amazing but what he does. Still I must keep my distance and remember my position.
The authorities are against this man and say he is a heretic and they must be right. It is difficult though because the people are on his side. Even my wife listens to what he is saying.
My little girl, though I can't call her that much longer as she will be a woman by her next birthday, she thinks he is wonderful. Little good it has done her as she is so ill. Do you know she even wants me to go and see Jesus to ask him to come and make her well again.
"I can't do that" I said to her, "What would people say if I, the President of the Elders, were to go to this man. They would take my job away. I have a position to uphold, dignity to preserve."

Veronica My name is Veronica. For years now I have suffered heavy bleeding and as you know I am not even allowed to go into the outer chamber of the Synagogue because I am regarded as unclean. In fact I am not supposed to mix with other people at all.
I have tried every remedy known. Doctor after doctor has given me their cures but as they got rich I have steadily got worse. I wasn't able to work and I am a constant embarrassment to my family. I am weak all the time from the loss of blood. I am so alone and afraid.
My daughter tells me that Jesus is coming here again. She says "Perhaps he can heal you mum. It would be so good if you could be free again."

Short break (Prayers for the sick might be used here)

Jairus My daughter is at death's door. I don't know what to do! She keeps asking for Jesus to come and make her better. My wife wants me to go but would Jesus want to help me? They say he is coming to the lakeside but there will be so many people there. If I go they will all see me, but if I don't go then my poor child will die without her last wish being granted and my wife would never forgive me. O God what should I do?

Veronica He is coming, but all these people! I shall get into so much trouble if they see me. How can I tell him what is wrong in front of everyone and him a man as well. Perhaps if I can just touch him, even the edge of his cloak that will be enough. He won't know and I can then slip away unnoticed. That's what I will do, just a touch of his cloak. That will be enough. O God help me, you are my only hope.

Short break in which a hymn such as Father I place into your hands could be sung

Jairus I did it! I went to Jesus in spite of all the crowds around him. I could imagine the shock on their faces when I turned up especially after all the things I have had to say about him.

But I couldn't see anything except Jesus and I felt so ashamed at how I had spoken against him; so sorry that I had taken so long to do what my little girl wanted me to do. My servants pushed the crowds aside telling them to make way for me. As I reached the water's edge I fell to my knees and begged him to come with me.

"Jesus" I cried, "my daughter is very ill. Please come and place your hands on her so that she will get well and live."

He climbed down from the boat and stood in front of me. "Stand up Jairus, I will come with you." I was so thrilled as we passed through the crowd to my home until suddenly he stopped and said "Who touched me? I couldn't believe it, there were hundreds of people there milling about and he said "Who touched me"!

Veronica Sorry! That was me. I was so desperate but I didn't want to make a fuss. I thought that if I could just touch one of the tassels on his cloak I could be healed. I had to be close enough and I only just managed to flick one of the tassels. That's when he stopped and asked "Who touched me?"

I nearly died on the spot. I heard one of the disciples saying "Don't be silly, they are all touching you!" But I knew it was me that he wanted. He just stood there and waited for me to own up. I knew by the feeling in my body that I was cured so I fell at his feet.

All this time poor Jairus was pacing up and down, worried about his little girl. Jesus took my hand, "Stand up" he said. Then he looked into my eyes, such a look of tenderness, and said "My daughter, your faith has made you whole. Go in peace and be healed of your trouble."

I was filled with such warmth and joy that I cried out Alleluia, alleluia.

Jairus It was frustrating to wait for this woman. I wasn't used to it, but then matters got worse as one of my servants came from the house. "Come home master" he said, "There is no need to trouble Jesus any more for you daughter is dead." I can't describe how awful those words were for me, but then Jesus touched me, "Don't be afraid Jairus, she is only sleeping."

For some reason I believed him and we continued to the house where the mourners were already weeping and wailing. My poor wife was absolutely distraught."

Jesus held his hand up "What is all this fuss about. The girl is not dead, she is only sleeping."

They began to laugh at him but we chased them out of her room and Jesus went over to her bed side and held her hand. He spoke so quietly "Little girl, it is time to wake up. Come I want you to get up now."

The scene as she did so was amazing. Everyone was astounded when they saw her walking. And she was so happy when she saw Jesus that she went straight to him and they hugged each other. Then she came to me and hugged me, "Thank you daddy" she said, "I knew Jesus would find you."

I thought then that she had just got her words the wrong way round but I think she knew what she was saying because Jesus did find me and we were all healed that day.

A prayer for the year Every

Glory be to God, every where, every day, every one.
Glory be to the Father the Son and the Holy Spirit;
creation, salvation and inspiration.
God of all places, for all time and for all people.

Everywhere God, we give you thanks and praise,
for you are with us everywhere we go,
nowhere is beyond your grace and love,
and yet we try to hide from you
when we are ashamed of what we have done.

Forgive us we pray for we are not always worthy of your love.
There are places where we doubt your presence
and therefore deny your power.
Be with us we pray wherever we may be, at home, at work,
at school or college, in the street and the shop,
Everywhere God we praise you.

Everyday God, we give you thanks and praise
for you are with us at all times,
from our waking to our sleeping.
There is no time when we cannot turn to you
yet we do forget that you are with us.

Stay with us we pray at all times,
a prayer to bless the night, a song to greet the day,
in times of joy and of sorrow,
in ordinary moments of work or relaxation.

Forgive us we pray for we do get things wrong.
There are times when we are afraid or depressed
and do not turn to you,
times when we feel guilty about what we have done
or not done. Everyday God we praise you.

Everyone God, we give you our thanks and praise,
for you are in all the people that we will meet.
Nobody is beyond your mercy
or unworthy of your love and ours.

But we do reject people who are different to ourselves;
we allow our ingrained prejudices to deny your presence
in the face of those unknown to us.

Forgive us we pray because we still reject you.
We are afraid of strangers,
critical of those who do things that are wrong,
too ready to make judgements
and unwilling to forgive those who have hurt us

Remind us we pray that you are present in everyone,
the smile of friendship, the touch of companionship,
the wildness of a child, the willingness to make your peace,
to be your love, to share your joy.
Everyone God we praise you.

Glory be to God whose love fills our lives.

Introduction to the writer

This is Colin's third book of worship material. 'Give me a Voice Lord' has long since sold out and 'Sharing Jesus', a collection of fifty new hymns which came out last year is well on the way. This collection of material is designed to show how wide a range of poetry, prayer and thought provoking meditation there can be.

Born in Perth (Scotland) and educated at Tiffin School in Kingston, Colin has been married to Janet for fifty years, and they have four children and six grandchildren. He has been involved in lay preaching ever since he was asked at the age of nineteen by the local Air Force Chaplain to go to a little Methodist chapel in North Yorkshire.

On leaving the R.A.F. he worked in the Bank of England for nearly ten years and helped in the running of a church based open youth club in Battersea until in 1967 he felt called to work in the Probation Service. In 1979 the family moved to Reading where he is a member and elder of St Andrew's United Reformed Church.

In this book he has dipped into his own experiences and into the characters he has met during nearly thirty years as a probation officer working in South Lambeth, Battersea, Holloway prison and in Berkshire. For the last twelve years before he retired he worked as a family mediator.

He began writing hymns when working with a youth preaching team and from that began nearly forty years of writing worship material, especially new hymns. His work has been published in many anthologies and he is a regular contributor to 'Worship Live'. All of it has been used by him in both the United Reformed and Methodist churches in which he regularly preaches. In his poems and prayers his experience of working in places of deep need shows and gives them a depth of understanding and feeling for those who are 'Seeking Jesus' and those who Jesus is seeking.